This book belongs to:

Auslan family signs
Auslan mealtime signs
Auslan weather signs
Auslan colours signs
Auslan shapes signs
Auslan animals signs

Auslan: Parts of the Hand

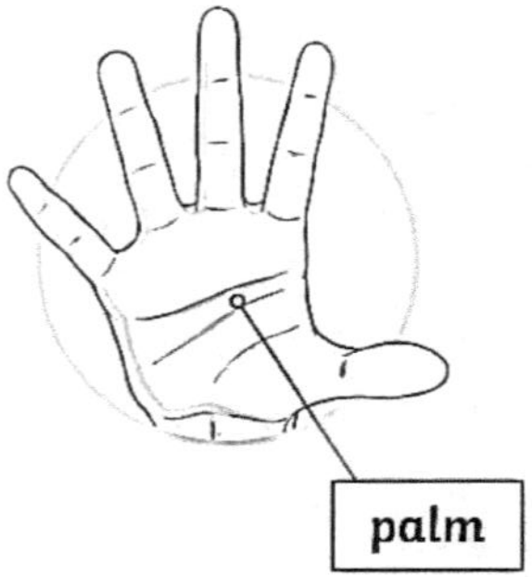

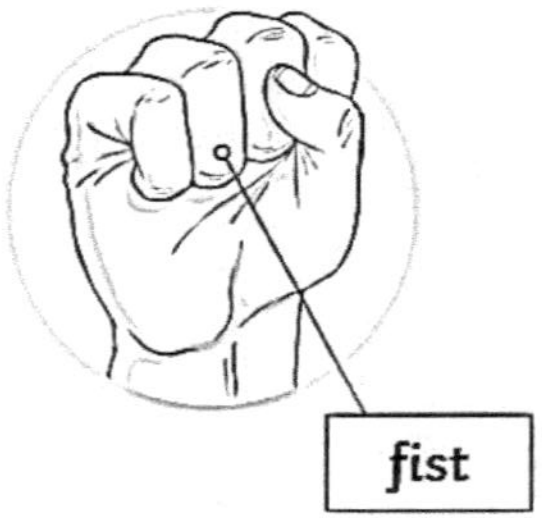

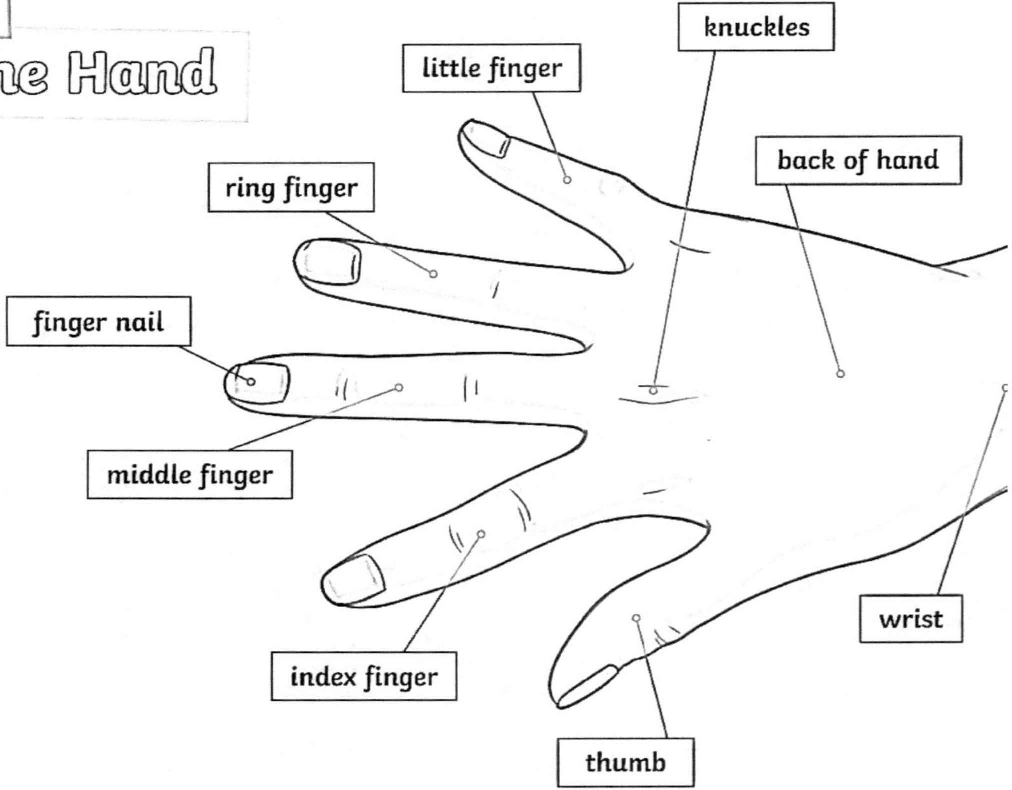

Family

Mum

Mother

Dad

Father

Sister

Brother

Grandfather

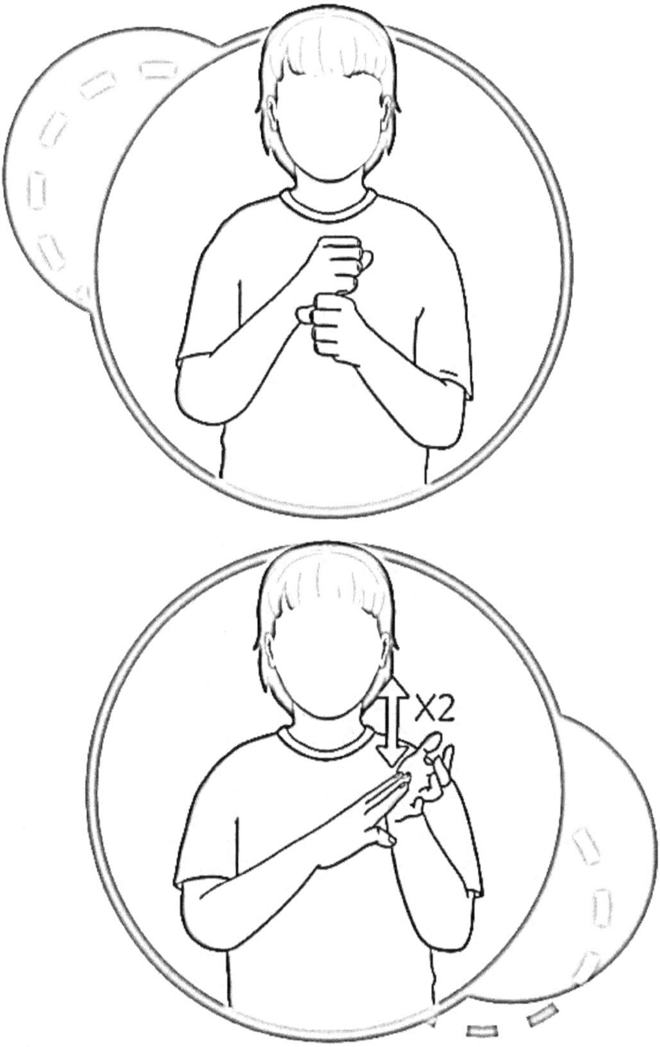

Grandmother

Step-mum

Step-dad

Auntie

Uncle

Cousin

Niece

Nephew

Partner

Fiancee

Friend

Auslan mealtime signs

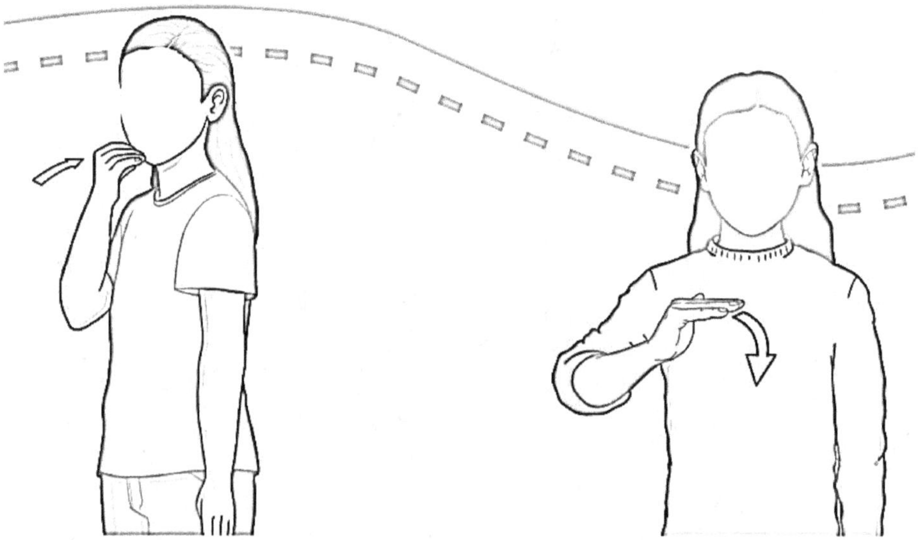

Eat/meal

Table

Chair

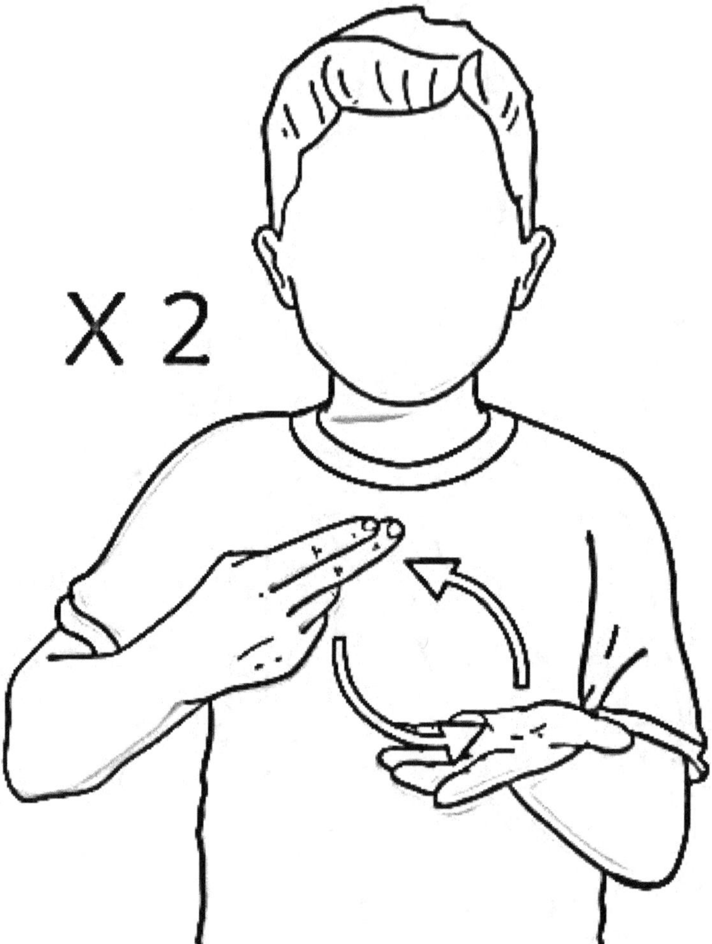

Breakfast

Lunch

Dinner

Plate

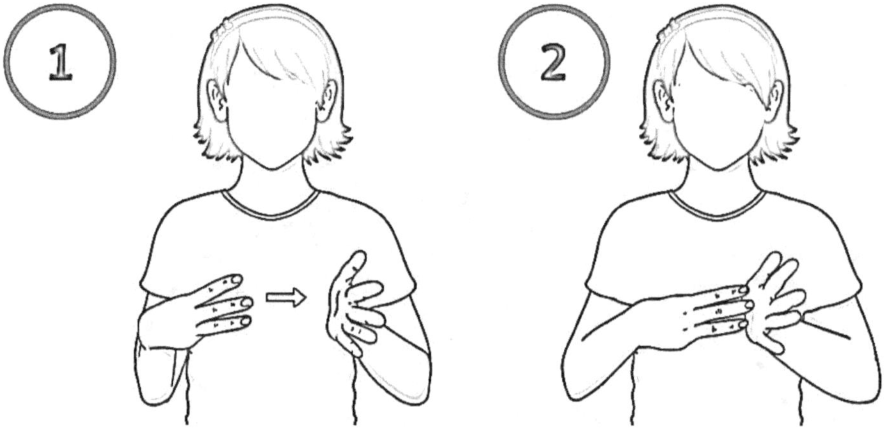

Fork

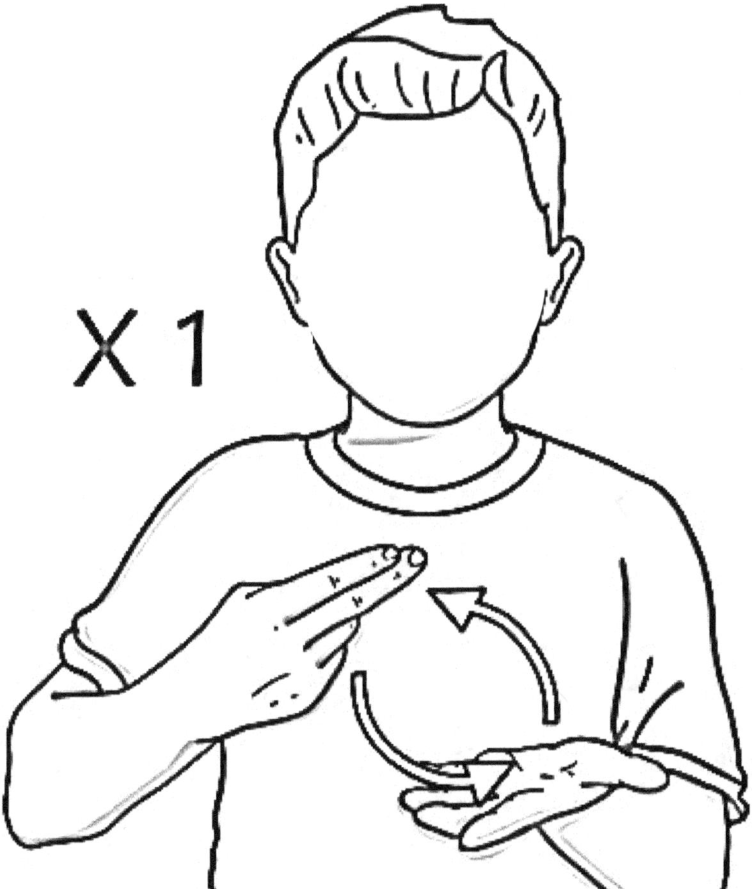

Spoon

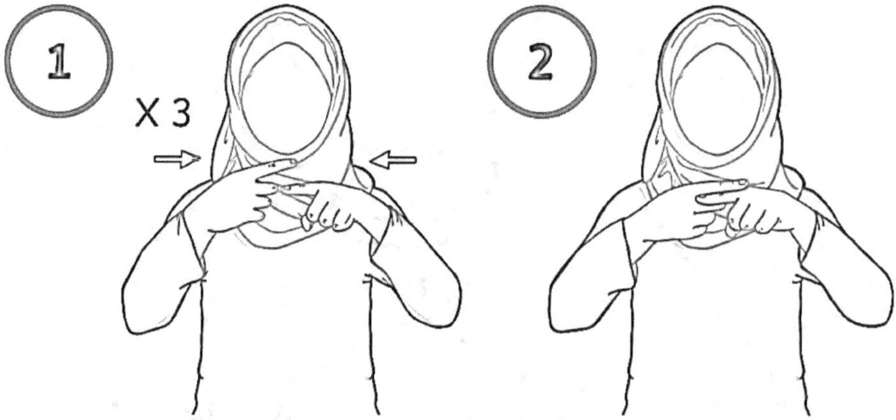

Knife

Auslan weather signs

Weather

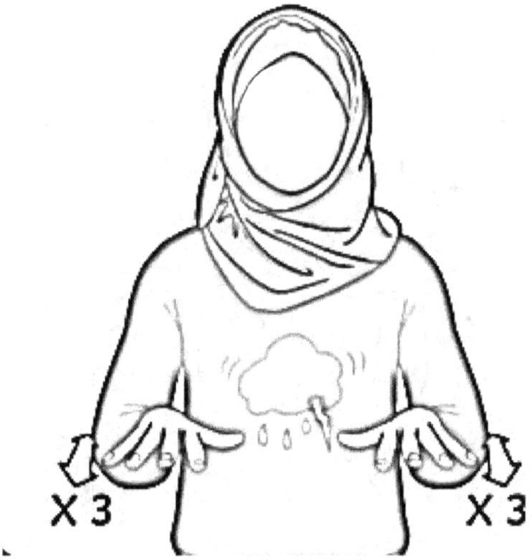

Thunder

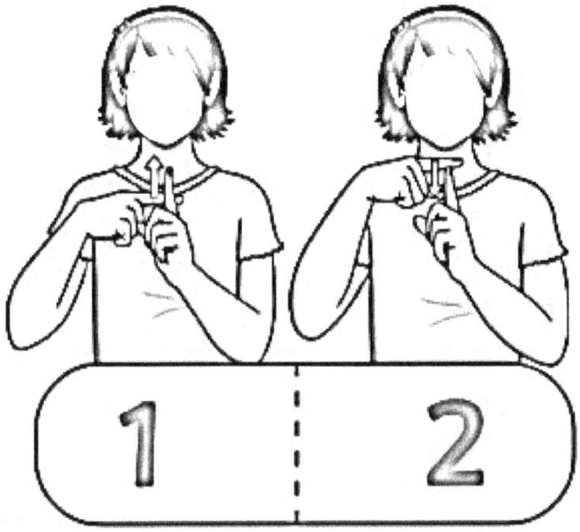

Temperature

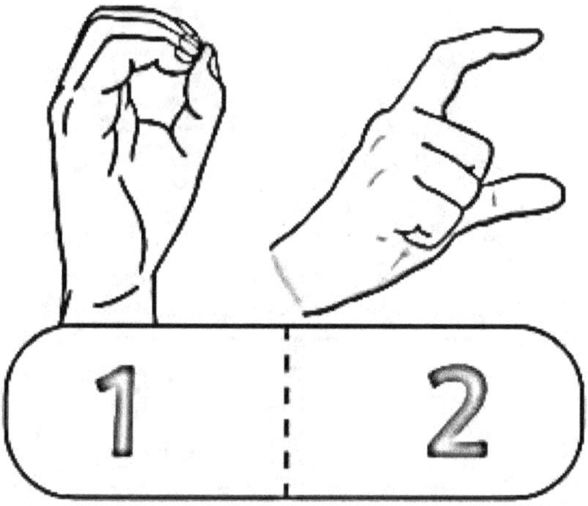

Degrees Celsius

Rainbow

Warm

Freezing

Hot

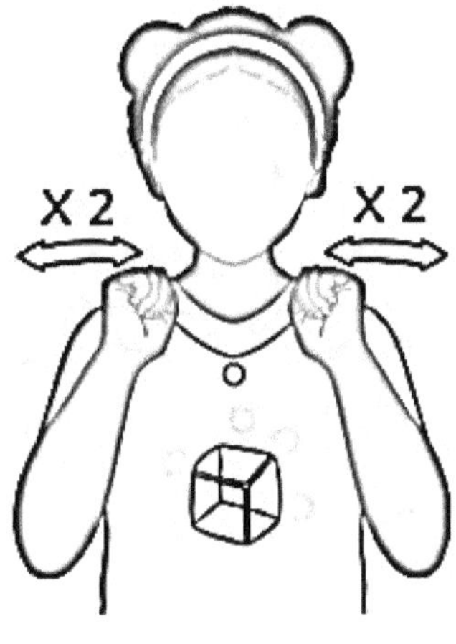

Cold

Sun

Rain

Snow

Clouds

Wind

Lightning

Auslan colours signs

White

Black

Brown

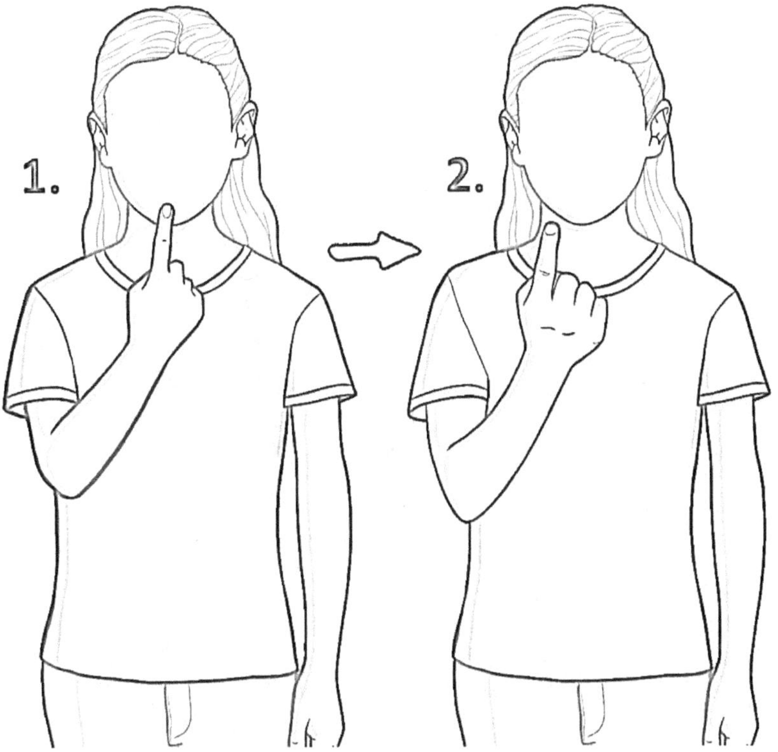

Pink

Purple

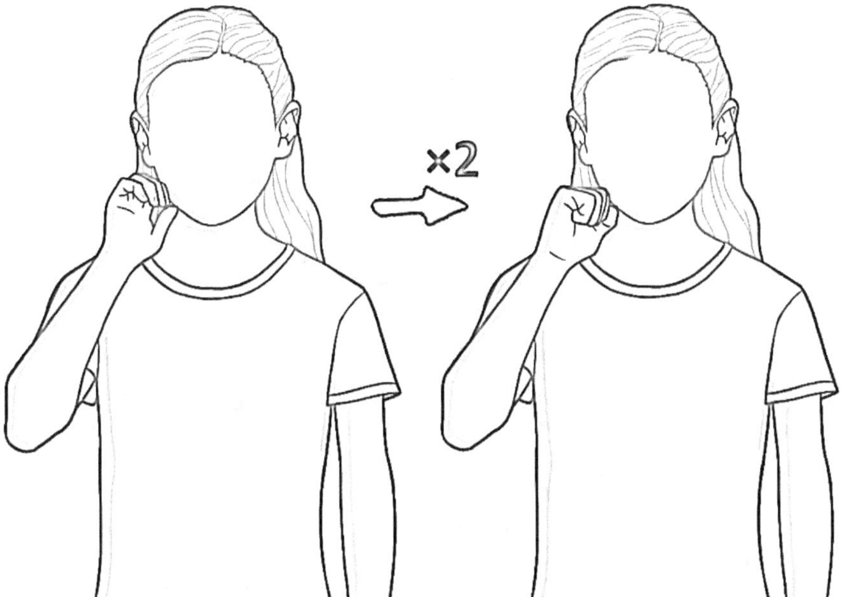

Orange

Green

Red

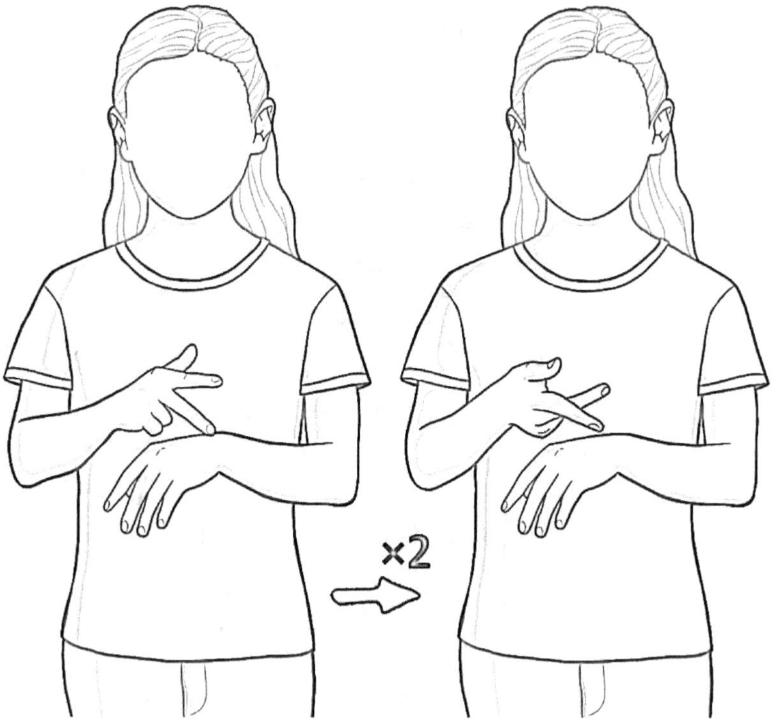

Blue

Auslan shapes signs

Shape

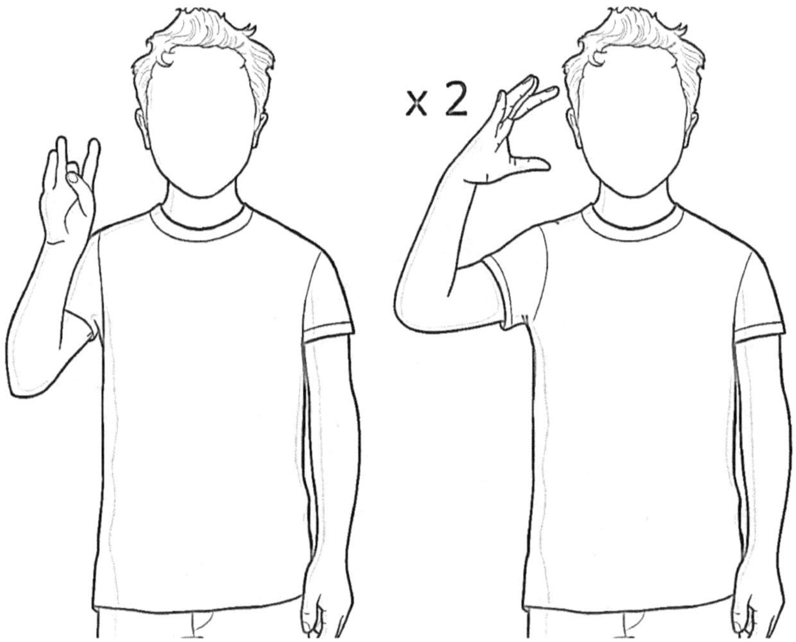

Star

Rectangle

Diamond

Circle

Square

Triangle

Auslan animals signs

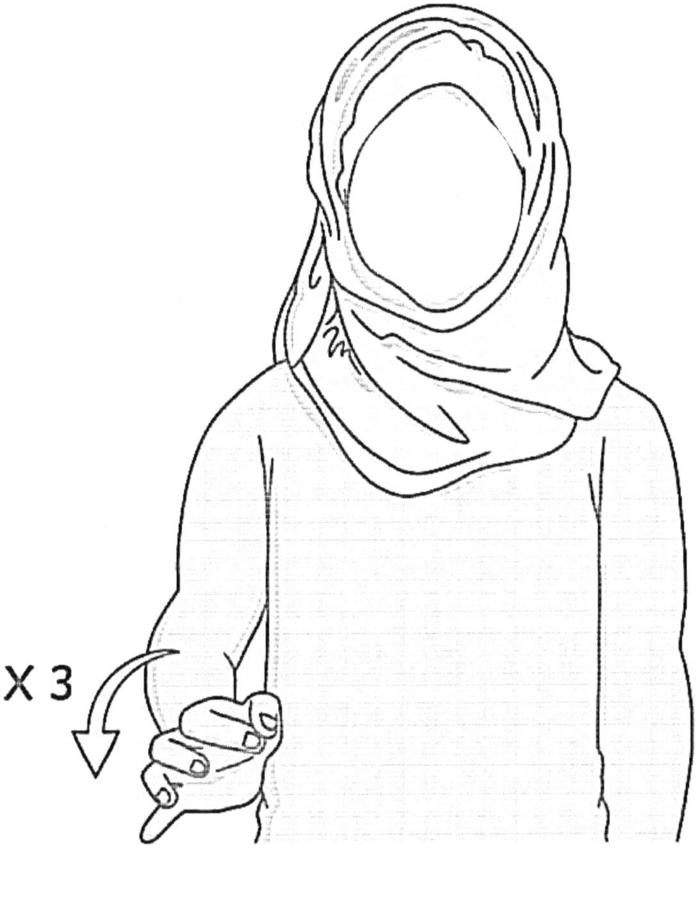

Dog

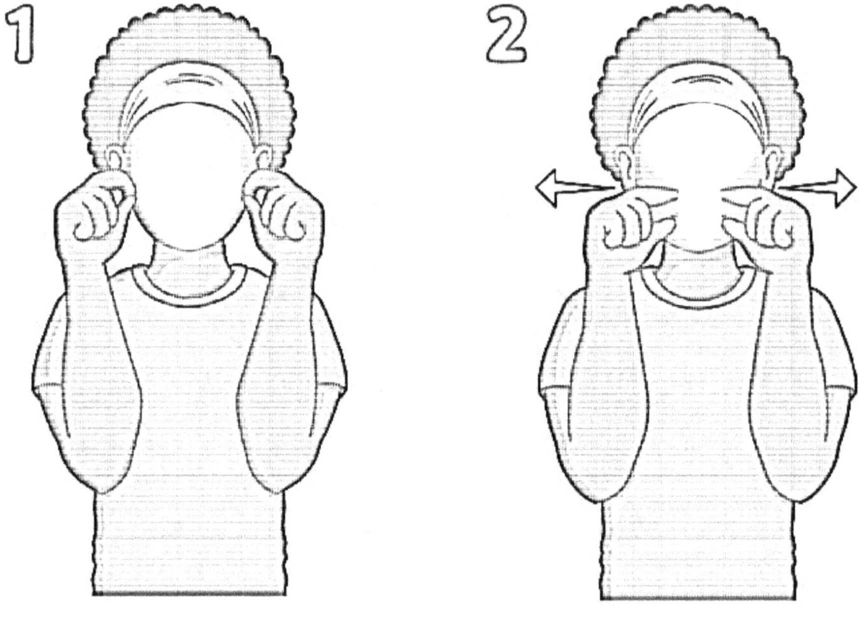

Cat

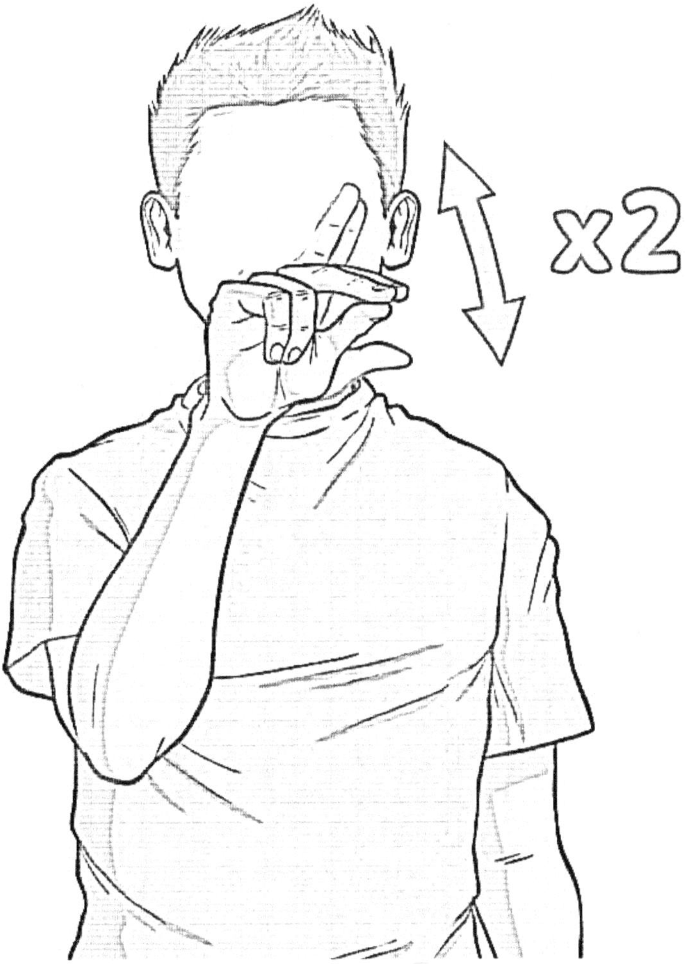

Duck

Cow

Horse

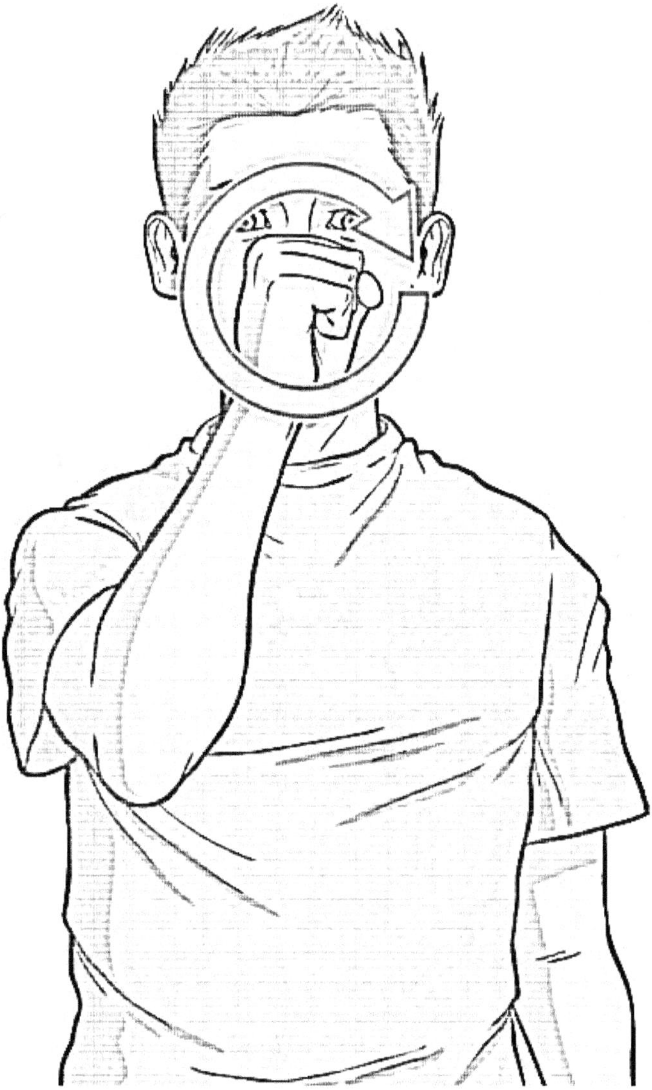

Pig

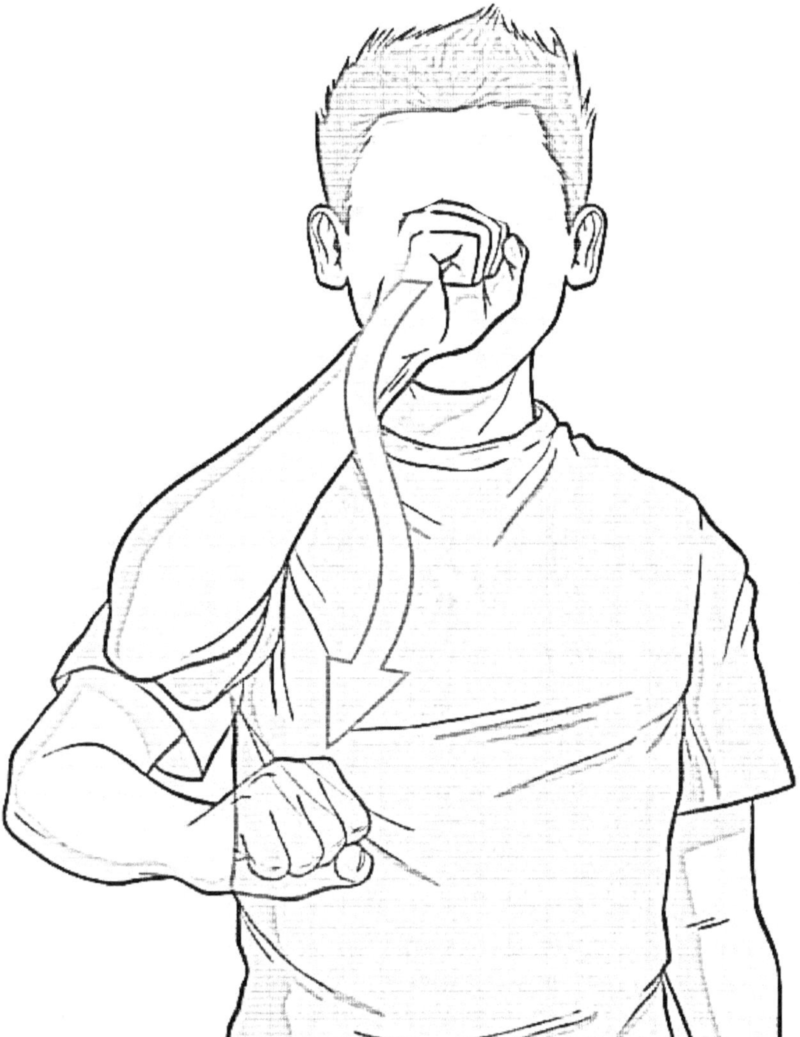

Elephant

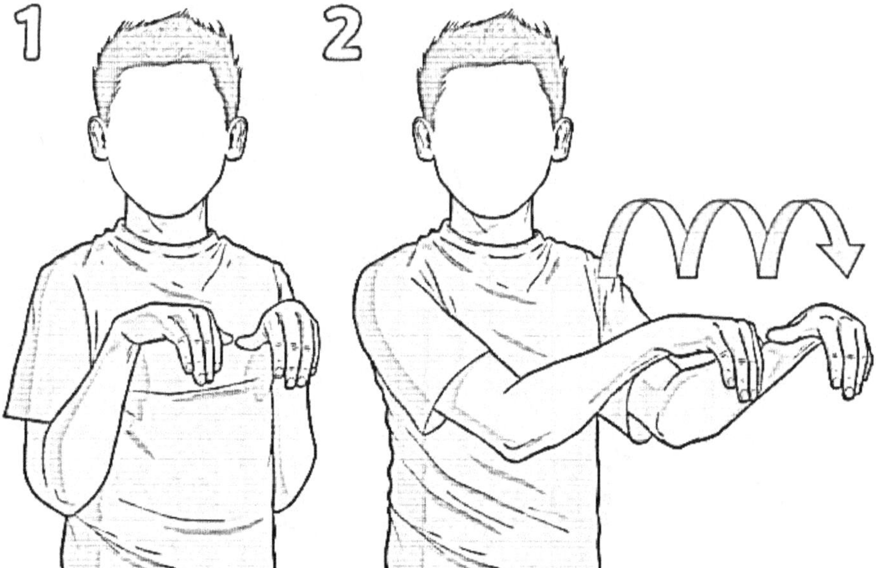

Kangaroo

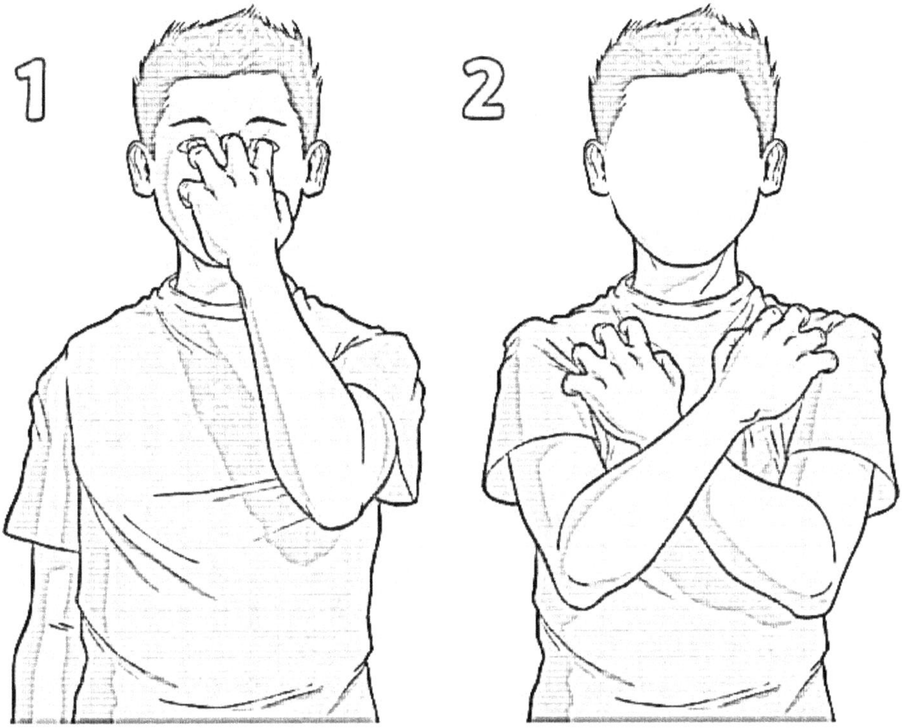

Koala

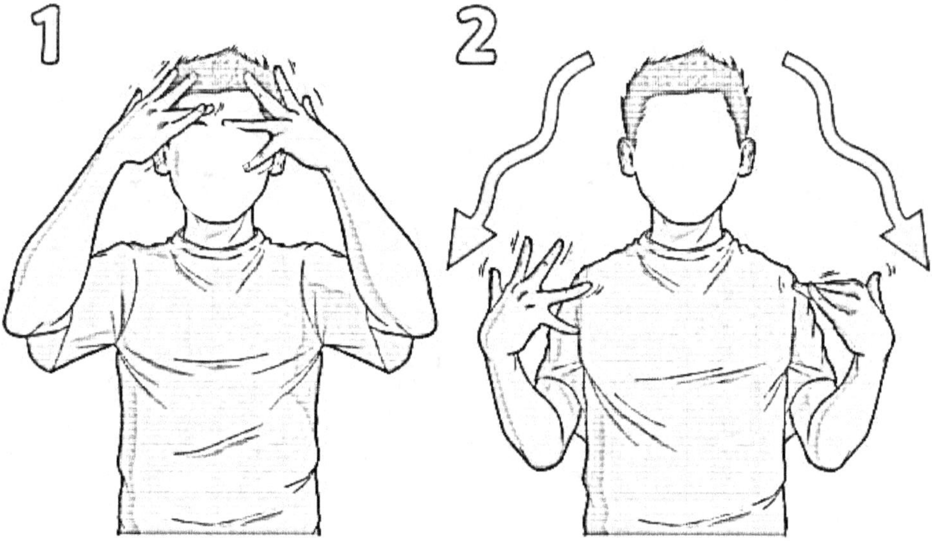

Lion

Crocodile

1

2

Wombat

Echidna

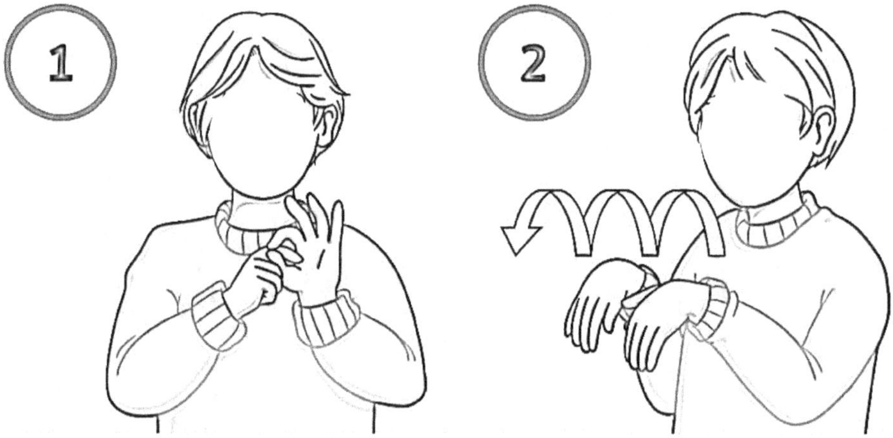

Quokka

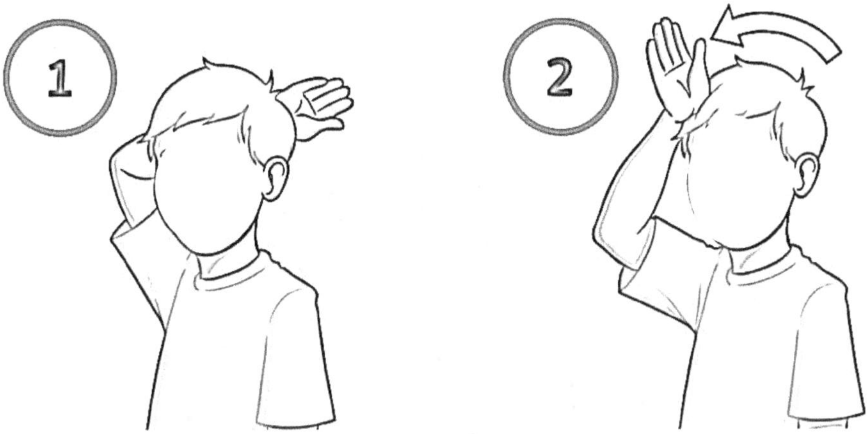

Cockatoo

Platypus

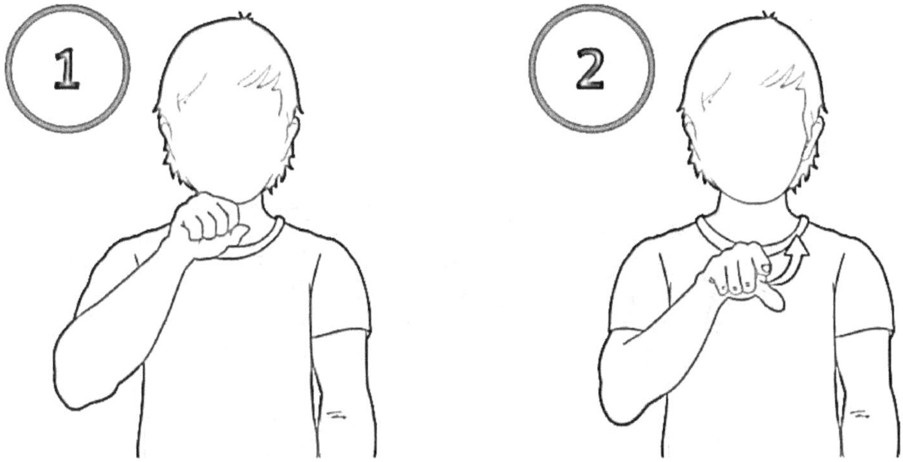

Lizard

Thank you!

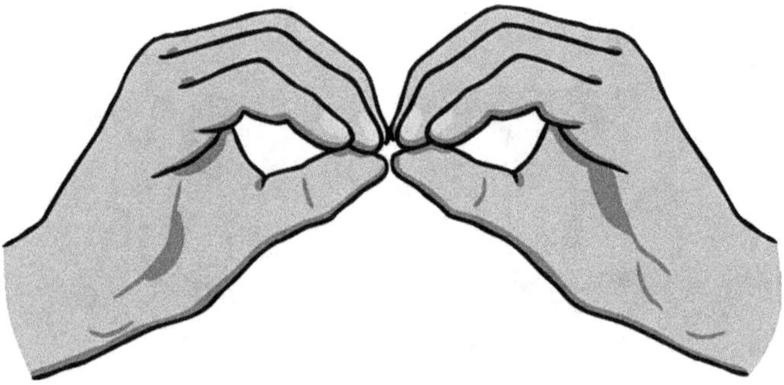

www.ingramcontent.com/pod-product-compliance
Lightning Source LLC
LaVergne TN
LVHW011737060526
838200LV00051B/3206
9780406082404